Notes on Titus

I0170951

Glen Burch

ISBN: 978-1-78364-487-2

www.obt.org.uk

****

The Open Bible Trust
Fordland Mount, Upper Basildon,
Reading, RG8 8LU, UK.

Notes on Titus

Contents

Introduction

Introduction

Paul's letter to Titus, together with 1 and 2 Timothy, form what are commonly known as the Pastoral Epistles. First called "Pastoral" in the eighteenth century, they were given this label because they emphasize pastoring responsibilities. However, it might be more accurate to call them the Leadership Epistles, because leadership is addressed here on many fronts: personal, parental, spousal, generational, pastoral, evangelistic and apostolic. Much more could be written about the Epistle to Titus than space will afford in these pages; with all the emphasis on the believer's walk, the practical applications might easily fill a large volume. This set of *Notes on Titus* will be limited to a more fundamental treatment of the issues concerned and will attempt to point out any dispensational characteristics present.

Background on the Person of Titus

As with the other two Pastoral Epistles, the book of Titus is formally addressed to a single individual. Nevertheless, it would not be incorrect to classify all three books as "both semi-personal and semi-ecclesiastic"[1]. Although the tone of the letters is personal, the doctrinal lessons have a wider application and are intended for the whole church. Paul's final word in Titus, "grace be with you all", makes it clear that a wider readership was intended than just Titus.

There is no mention of Titus' conversion in any of the New Testament books, but his accompaniment on Paul's journey to Jerusalem in A.D. 51 to settle the Gentile question (Galatians 2:1-3; Acts 15:1-2) makes him an early fellow-worker. He was a Greek (Galatians 2:3) and may have become affiliated with Paul during his first journey through Cyprus or Galatia, or even while at Paul's home base of Cilician Antioch. Titus may have accompanied Paul on his second missionary journey and subsequent travels, but he is not even mentioned in Acts. Apparently he had special missions as Paul's envoy to the church at Corinth (2 Corinthians 7:6-7; 13-15; 8:16-17, 23; 12:18), and later as his emissary to

---

[1] 1 Timothy 2:1-4; 3:14-16; 4:7-8; 5:3-4; 6:3-6,10-11; 2 Timothy 3:1-5,10-12

Crete (Titus 1:5). In view of the fractiousness of both the Corinthian and the Cretan churches (1 Corinthians 1:11-12; 3:3; 6:1-8; Titus 1:10-13) it appears that Titus was something of a spiritual troubleshooter, able to be just as tough-minded as the situation demanded.

The bond between Paul and Titus was especially strong. Paul calls Titus his "partner" and "fellow-worker", a brother without whom he could find no rest (2 Corinthians 8:23; 2:13). In Titus 1:4 Paul even addresses him as his "genuine child according to the common faith". One might surmise whether Titus was a convert of Paul's, but the apostle used similar words of Timothy in 1 Timothy 1:2. If Timothy was known to Paul previous to his selecting him for service in Acts 16:1, it is not mentioned. I am left with the impression that both Timothy and Titus were adopted children of faith, so to speak, and not direct converts of Paul's.

After the close of the Acts period, what can be reliably known of Titus must be gleaned from the Pastoral Epistles. Titus went to Crete with Paul, who left him there to build up the church leadership and set things in order (Titus 1:5). Titus' stewardship after this seems to take a dark turn. If 2 Timothy follows Titus chronologically, as is commonly held, then 2 Timothy 4:10 gives us the last word on Titus.

> ... for Demas forsook me, having loved the present age, and went to Thessalonica, Crescens to Galatia, Titus to Dalmatia.

The words "Titus to Dalmatia" tell us his last known destination, but this is an incomplete statement and an ellipsis must be supplied from the first part of the verse: "Demas forsook me". Some will find it difficult to imagine Titus as having abandoned Paul in departing to Dalmatia. Apparently Demas must bear the brunt of Paul's criticism because desertion and love of the present age are attributed directly to him. But the sentence runs on without a break, telling where Crescens and Titus went also; and thus it may be that Paul intended to tar them with the same brush. If this conclusion is correct, it may be that the same strong mindedness that enabled Titus to deal with the unruly Cretans and Corinthians led to willfulness and stumbling in the end. It is curious that there is no mention of Titus in the book of Acts, considering how close he was to Paul's ministry.

Surely Luke must have known him personally. Luke wrote Acts at least two years after Paul's house arrest in Rome, but we cannot be certain how long after the Acts period closed. Acts finishes without even a hint as to Paul's intentions after the house arrest the account just ends abruptly. This may or may not signify the point at which Acts was published. If Luke were to have written Acts later, after Titus' departure to Dalmatia, it may have proved beneficial for a church threatened by disarray and schism to leave unmentioned one who now contributed to that disarray. On the other hand Titus may have had legitimate church matters to attend to in Dalmatia, while it had been Paul's judgment to assign him higher priority work elsewhere. How to prioritize our labors (spiritual and otherwise) is a wisdom we all need to cultivate.

Authorship
and
Dating

Authorship and Dating

The authenticity of the Pastoral Epistles has been attacked more vehemently than any of the other Pauline books. However, in the early church the Pastorals were universally accepted as being of Paul and were held in high esteem as the authoritative word of God. Paul names himself as the author and addresses personal comments to two colleagues by name. For those who believe in the inerrancy of Scripture, as I hope the reader does, this should prove sufficient to establish authorship.

Pseudonymous works were in abundance in post apostolic times, but epistolary material would have been very difficult to imitate. The Biblical pretenders tended to be gospels, acts and apocalypses rather than epistles.

One objection that is sometimes put forward is our inability to place the personal details of the Pastoral Epistles within the historical framework of Acts. But Acts makes no claim to be the complete biography of Paul's apostleship. Also the book ends rather abruptly after Paul's two year house arrest in Rome, and the opportunity for a visit to Crete with Titus could have followed this period of detention.

Some have contended that the high degree of church organization indicated in the Pastorals belongs to the second rather than the first century. But careful examination reveals no more organization than the criteria needed for selecting pastors and their assistants, and the exercise of their basic responsibilities. The selection process was carried out by Christ appointed apostles and evangelists, like Timothy and Titus, the same as it was during Acts (14:23). There is nothing here that does not accord with the first century.

Those who deny Paul's authorship of the Pastoral Epistles tend to date the books in the late first or early second centuries. Some of them believe that the main purpose of these letters was to combat fully developed, second century Gnosticism. But an incipient form of Gnosticism existed in the first century. The book of Colossians addresses perverse practices such as asceticism (Colossians 2:21-23), which later became much in vogue among the various Gnostic schools.

Having faith in the authenticity of the Pastorals and being unable to fit them into the Acts chronology, we can accept a probable date for Titus between 63 and 68 A.D. Paul was a free man when he wrote the Epistle to Titus, so his time of house arrest in Rome must have come to an end (Acts 28:30). His release probably preceded the onset of the Neronian persecution (64 A.D.), because so notable a Christian "ringleader" as Paul would hardly have been freed while lesser known believers were being savagely executed.

After his release from confinement at Rome, Paul journeyed again to the Aegean region. He left Titus in Crete (Titus 1:5) and asked Timothy to remain at Ephesus while he headed for Macedonia (1 Timothy 1:3). Later he expected to spend the winter at Nicopolis, where Titus was to join him (Titus 3:12). He also looked for an opportunity to pay Timothy a visit, presumably after winter (1 Timothy 3:14). The request in Titus 3:13 for Titus to send along Zenas the lawyer and Apollos (presumably the orator of Acts 18:24) may signal continuing legal problems with the Empire. Those problems apparently caught up with him as he journeyed in Timothy's direction. He appears to have been arrested near Troas, where his baggage was left (2 Timothy 4:13), and he was taken back to Rome (2 Timothy 1:16-17).

Overview
of the Book

Overview of the Book

The following outline embodies my best judgment of what the book of Titus is about.

A Opening greeting, with doctrinal statement (1:1-4)

  B Titus dispatched with a mission to fulfill (1:5-8)

    C The faithful word and those who contradict it (1:9-16)

      D Sound speech: teaching about right conduct (2:1-10)

        E Work of Christ contrasted with works of man (2:11-14)

      D Commanding speech: exhortation to right conduct (2:15-3:2)

      E Work of Christ contrasted with works of man (3:3-5)

    C The faithful word and those who content against it (3:8-11)

  B Titus summoned and given a mission (3:12-14)

A Closing greeting (3:15)

As in all of his Epistles, Paul opens and closes with personal greetings (items A. and *A*.). The teachings of the book of Titus are mainly pragmatic, dealing with unique responsibilities assigned to Titus (items B. and *B*.) and with the more general responsibility of a faithful walk (items C. and *C*.). Conflict and contradiction are to be expected by those who keep faith with the sound doctrine. The natural enmity between flesh and spirit is the root of this conflict. Although the Enemy is spiritual in nature, rather than blood and flesh (Ephesians 6:12), we know we shall have conflict with those who are influenced by "the god of this age" (2 Corinthians 4:4; Ephesians 2:1-3). Before faith converted us, our nature was one of hostility toward God and His followers (see items E. and *E*.). Therefore, now that we are His followers we can expect to be under pressure in this world (2 Timothy 3:12). Responding to this hostile yet alluring environment in which Christians find themselves, the sound teaching (items D. and *D*.) must consist of both positive and negative elements: positive about things of the spirit, but negative about things of the flesh leading to sin.

Thus the Epistle to Titus gives us an appropriate balance between positive teaching and admonition. We should be wary of an easy Christianity that lacks admonition, for it will leave the door ajar for sin to creep back into our lives. But the word of God was designed to be "profitable for teaching, for conviction, for correction, for discipline in righteousness", so that the man of God might be complete (2 Timothy 3:16-17). The negative aspects of conviction, correction and discipline are just as needful as the positive aspect of teaching. If we are to attain our inheritance (reward) in God's kingdom it will be mainly on the basis of keeping a faithful walk, having put off all the wicked deeds of the flesh (Ephesians 5:3-13).

Titus
Chapter 1

Titus Chapter 1

Paul opens his letter to Titus with an expansive greeting, exceeded in size only by his greetings in Romans and Galatians. This opening, like several others, contains both a defense of Paul's apostleship and some affiliated doctrinal remarks. The Epistle to Titus is noteworthy in that Paul defends his stewardship first on the basis of its relationship to the truth, and secondly on the basis of its divine origin. In his other epistles he gives the greater emphasis to his selection by the Lord Jesus Christ. But in Titus his relationship to the faith of God's elect (the church) and to the godliness truth is put forth as the primary reason for his evangelizing activity. This shift in emphasis foreshadowed a time when Paul's message would have to stand alone so to speak, independent of an apostolic regime which was about to draw to a close. The same sense of priority comes through in Paul's urging Timothy (2 Timothy 1:8) neither to be ashamed of the testimony (first) nor of him (second).

In Titus, as in the Pastorals generally, we find brief references to doctrinal matters whose substance must be gleaned from other Scriptures. For example, the teaching about salvation in 2:11-14 and 3:4-7 is fundamental. It might even be described as "pithy", lacking dispensational embellishments. Paul gives Titus no detailed foundational or dispensational basis for such terms as "the faith of God's elect ones" (1:1), "the truth in harmony with godliness" (1:1), "the preaching (literally, 'proclamation') which I was entrusted with" (1:3), "the common faith" (1:4), "the faithful word in harmony with the doctrine" (1:9), "the sound teaching" (1:9; 2:1), "the faith" (1:13; 3:15), "the truth" (1:14), "the word of God" (2:5), and "the teaching of our Saviour God" (2:10). Many of these expressions relate chiefly to practical issues: that is, the outworking of truth in believers' lives. Titus' keen personal grasp of the doctrinal foundations, like that of the other intended readers, made it unnecessary to embellish these simple references to truth.

What "the faith" is about in Titus can be inferred from a few dispensational remarks found in the book. For example, in the opening greeting Paul mentions the hope of eternal life which God promised "before the world began" (literally "before age-times"). Analogously 2 Timothy 1:9 informs us

Notes on Titus   27

that God's grace was given to us in Christ Jesus "before age-times".

When we read in Ephesians 1:4 of our election by God "before the foundation (lit. 'overthrow') of the world", we can recognize the same teaching in somewhat different words. The Epistle to the Ephesians provides a necessary foundation on which to erect the practical teaching of Titus.

Ephesians 3:1-9 makes it clear that the gospel secret of Paul's later ministry had not been revealed to the sons of men at any time in the past. It had remained completely hidden until Israel failed nationally to receive her King and kingdom (Acts 28:23-31). Following the postponement of Israel's hope (not the "hope" of Titus 1:2), the revelation of another aspect of the redemptive work of Christ was sent to mankind. In this new "dispensation of the fullness of the seasons" (Ephesians 1:10) Christ has become Head of His body the church, a multiethnic church in which national heritage and privileges play no part whatsoever. This church has been called to a heavenly kingdom in the heavenly places where Christ now sits at the right hand of the Father.

The concept of a nation is genealogical, physical and earthbound; as such it is alien to the heavenly environment of our heritage. The Old Testament Scriptures deal exclusively with God's earthly plan, centered in Israel as His priestly nation. These earthly things are now in abeyance, and are irrelevant to the heavenly kingdom.

In ascribing the promise of eternal life to a period "before age-times", the Epistle to Titus aligns itself with the book of Ephesians and the election before the overthrow of the world (i.e., the overthrow of Genesis 1:2). Both a promise and a calling traceable to such ancient "before" times belong to God's kingdom "in the heavenlies", and to the church He calls to receive it. This is essentially what "the faith" is about in Titus.

We should not fail to take note of the only reference to "age-times" outside the Pastoral Epistles. This can be found in Romans, an Acts period epistle with the earthly kingdom in view:

> But to Him Who is able to strengthen you in harmony with my gospel and the proclamation of Jesus Christ, in harmony with the revelation

of a mystery silenced *during age-times*, but manifested now and by the prophetic Scriptures, in harmony with the commandment of the eternal God, made known for faith obedience unto all the nations. (Romans 16:25-26)

In Romans a mystery was revealed, a secret kept silent during age-times and yet concealed in the prophetic Scriptures. That secret concerned the faith obedience of the nations being found acceptable to God, apart from keeping the Law of Moses. Those nationals who lived by their faith were grafted into faithful Israel to share in her spiritual blessings (Romans 11:11-18). At the same time many in Israel were offended by the stumbling-stone of the gospel (11:25). The gospel that Paul preached to the nations in his early ministry had been promised before by the prophets (1:1-5), and yet the outworking of the gospel among Jews and Greeks remained a hidden aspect of Old Testament prophecy (see Paul's use of Hosea in Romans 9:25-26, and his use of Moses and Isaiah in Romans 10:18-21, for example).

The mysteries of Romans and Ephesians both emphasize the faith of Gentile believers. But in

Romans the Jew is still preeminent (1:16; 2:9), while in Ephesians the Jewish religion is passé. Although it lacks specificity, the gospel message of Titus is dispensationally different from that of Romans – each relates its message to different aspects of "age-times". We shall review more evidence of this in the section entitled "The Conflict with Judaism."

Godliness

In Titus 1:1 we find Paul basing his apostleship in part upon a recognition of truth based upon godliness.

> Paul, a servant of God and apostle of Jesus Christ, according to [the] faith of God's elect and [the] recognition of truth which is according to <u>godliness</u>.

We may infer from the many references to it that the "godly" life is an issue of keen importance in the Pastorals. Godliness in the root sense of the Greek word used (*eusebeia*) means literally to worship well or to rightly reverence. In its New Testament applications the term has nothing to do with formal worship. It applies rather to our day-to-day actions and attitudes, as reflections of our reverence toward God. For example, the care of one's aging parent is equated with being godly (*eusebeō*) in 1 Timothy 5:4. So the truth based on godliness is not some dry intellectual truth, but truth which engages one's whole being and leads to an attitude of reverence for all that God has planned for us. If we are truly His to command, then a spirit of godliness will be evident in us.

The other "godliness" passage in Titus personifies God's grace as our instructor in the godly life.

> For the grace of God appeared as a saving instrument for all men, instructing us that, having denied ungodliness and worldly passions, we should live soberly and righteously and <u>godly</u> in the present age. (Titus 2:11-12)

Our training in the godly life has been initiated through the heart of the "new man" within. It is only by the indwelling spirit of Christ that we can put off the "old man", and this we do when we deny ourselves indulgence in the sinful attitudes and passions that stir within us. *Eusebeia* and its various cognate forms appear more frequently in the Timothy letters than in Titus, and the informed reader would do well to read these passages also[2]. The relationship between godliness and the hidden inner life of the church, as summed up in "the mystery of godliness" (1 Timothy 3:16), is a subject I have explored elsewhere[3].

At the top of Paul's agenda in writing to Titus was his concern for Titus' mission in Crete. In verse five Paul wastes no time in reminding him of his responsibility toward the churches of Crete. Paul's care for his spiritual "son" was parental in nature and need not imply any laxity on Titus' part. Doubtless Titus had been well prepared for his mission there. But we parents are prone to remind our children of the obvious, because we are anxious for them. In this instance Paul was solicitous not only for Titus but also for the churches under his care.

_____

[2] *The Mystery of Godliness*, G. Burch, Open Bible Trust

[3] See 1 Timothy 1:10; 6:3; 2 Timothy 1:13; 4:3

The criteria for eldership spelled out by Paul may seem a bit relaxed to us today.

> If any is blameless, husband of one wife, having believing children, not under accusation of debauchery or insubordinate. For it behooves the overseer to be blameless as God's steward, not arrogant, not prone to anger, not given to wine, not contentious, not greedy, but hospitable, a lover of good, sober, just, holy, self-controlled, holding onto the faithful word according to the doctrine, that he may be able both to encourage with the sound teaching and to convict those who contradict. (Titus 1:6-9)

In the Cretan leadership situation the basic Christian virtues were what was needed most. And it was not sufficient that an overseer merely assent to such virtues; he had to live up to them blamelessly. Seeing that contemporary Cretan society abounded in liars and lazy gluttons (verse 12), it may have been something of an accomplishment for Christians there to maintain blameless conduct. The only academic requirement for an elder was adherence to God's faithful word, with the implied ability to use that word to exhort, teach and convict (verse 9). This standard was at variance with Paul's religious roots in Judaism, where recognition of one's authority depended upon affiliation with one of the rabbinical schools. Today many Christians would inquire of a man's Bible college or university affiliation before recognizing him as a teacher and leader in spiritual matters. We ought rather to review a man's Christian life as to whether it has been blameless, and then test his words against the word of God before accepting him as a pastor and teacher. See Appendix B for a broader treatment of the leadership offices in the early church.

The Conflict with Judaism

The remainder of chapter one takes up a theme of conflict and opposition. As usual the principal source of resistance to Paul's gospel was his former co-religionists, the Jews. On a first reading it is not clear whether "the circumcision" (verse 10) means converted or unconverted Jews. But their ability to enter Christian houses and overthrow them means that they must have been exclusively Christian converts! The enemy within is always the most insidious. Paul's statement in 2 Timothy 1:15 that all in Asia had turned away from him shows a growing Christian opposition to his leadership and teaching.

The point of view toward Judaism displayed in 1:10-16 is another dispensational key to the book of Titus. During Acts, while God was still dealing graciously with Israel, He allowed two different rules of conduct for some preachers of the gospel (1 Corinthians 9:19-22). Jewish ministers like Paul were free to deport themselves as Jews when ministering to the Jews, or as Greeks to the Greeks. God's covenant with the Jews had included many ordinances dealing with ritual purity, but these practices became just so many "Jewish fables" (Titus 1:14) in the new dispensation following the Acts period.

Although the Law was never meant as a means of salvation, faithfulness to its precepts (if carried out in the proper spirit) served to separate and prepare Israel for their unique role as the priestly nation. Paul had consistently taught that the Law, for all its benefits, could never render a man righteous (Galatians 2:16).

As a Jew among Jews there was no inconsistency in

his taking part in the Nazirite purification ceremony as late as Acts 21:20-24. But such an act would have been unthinkable after Acts 28, because God's favor no longer rested on a people practicing the Mosaic laws. This fact does not exclude Israelites or any other nationality from participating in God's program for today. Whoever truly believes God, has access to the heavenly kingdom. However, it is one thing to profess this belief, and perhaps another to practice it (Titus 1:16). Only those who live out "the faith of God's elect" and rightly divide His word of truth (2 Timothy 2:15) will God be pleased to call "faithful." And their faith will not include trusting in the ordinances of Judaism to please God.

The distinction between "pure" and "defiled" in Titus 1:15 (*KJV*) certainly goes beyond how the Law defines these terms. Avoiding the consumption of certain unclean animals or contact with dead bodies might have sufficed for mere legal purity, but purity in Titus is tantamount to believing and obeying all that God instructs His church to receive.

This instruction very definitely excludes the laws of ritual purity found in Judaism (Colossians 2:16-23; 1 Timothy 4:1-5; Titus 1:14-16). The pure are quite simply those who believe God, Who has purified them through the sacrifice of His Son (Titus 1:15; 2:14; Ephesians 5:25-27). During Acts there were two acceptable rules of conduct for believers. There were those who continued "all zealous of the Law" (Acts 21:20) and those with "the Law written in their hearts" (Romans 2:14-15). Although all things in themselves were pure at that time, those who were weaker in the faith (Jewish converts to Christianity) were given an accommodation (Romans 14:1-15:2). God was bending over backwards, as it were, to save all Israel. The Jew was first and foremost in His thoughts, and therefore a weak faithed dependence on the rituals of Judaism was tolerated.

But in the post Acts dispensation there should be no accommodation with Judaistic practices. Despite this truth a legalistic Christianity has gotten the upper hand, a situation anticipated by the warnings of Colossians chapter 2. The laissez-faire attitude toward diet and calendar observances prevalent during Acts (Romans 14:2-6) has given way to such stern warnings as: "let no one spoil you", "let no one judge you" and "let no one take away your prize" (Colossians 2:8,16,18). We must stand guard over ourselves lest we be drawn into the "touch not, taste not, handle not" world of ordinances and great showy doctrines of men (Colossians 2:20-23). To practice a Judaized Christian faith today is to reject God (Titus 1:16). Verse 16 contains much to reflect upon soberly.

We all profess to know God, but does our faith and walk reflect it? Does He perhaps find us abominable and "disobedient" (*apeithēs* conveys a rebellious mind, unwilling to be persuaded), because we fail to know Him as He would have us to know Him? Do we know Him through the word of truth rightly divided, as He commands us to (2 Timothy 2:15)? Or, like many Israelites during the time of their visitation, do we behave like "sons of disobedience" by clinging to what God has set aside while rejecting what He now offers? If we try today to assimilate any of Israel's covenant ordinances then we are disobeying God's word; for there is no precept of feast or food, no ritual and no ordinance, against which the body of Christ should be judged (Colossians 2:14-23).

Titus

Chapter 2

Titus Chapter 2

This section of the Epistle begins with a command for Titus to use "the sound teaching" in his guidance of the church. This is an echo of the instruction in 1:9 for elders to encourage their churches with "the sound teaching". Soundness in faith and in speech is the subject of three other passages in Titus (1:13-14; 2:2 and 2:7-8).

The Greek verb "to be sound" is *hugiainō*, which gives us our English "hygiene". The soundness or "health" of faith, speech, and teaching forms one of the main Pastoral Epistle themes (comparable to the "godliness" theme). By its usage, the word seems to have as much to do with moral as with doctrinal soundness, and even the doctrinal aspect has a practical slant to it.

The two references to soundness in 1:9-14 may have been meant to offset the moral laxity of Cretan society ("liars, evil beasts, lazy gluttons" in verse 12), in addition to countering the Judaistic ordinances that were polluting the consciences of some believers. In chapter two the contexts in which the word "sound" is found emphasize such practical virtues as sobriety, dignity, discretion, faithfulness, love, endurance, incorruption (i.e., purity or spirituality) and exemplary good works. It is possible that Paul does not fully describe "the sound teaching" either here or in the Timothy letters[4]. But it must have been well understood by the writer as well as the first readers what that teaching is. Perhaps the expression "sound teaching" should be taken as a watchword for all doctrine that applies to us today.

The force of the sound teaching in Titus 2:1 is applied to the conduct of various societal groups, beginning with the old men. The word for "old man" (*presbutēs*) is almost the same word as "elder" (*presbuteros*[5]) used in 1:5. Although the difference in words in Titus is sufficient to distinguish between

---

[4] Comparative of the adjective *presbus*, which was usually used as a noun for "old man" or "ambassador."

[5] Cp. 1 Timothy 5:1 where *presbuteros* describes old men generally.

these old men and the elders who lead the church[6], yet there remains a strong affinity between the two.

Older Christian men and women share with their overseers a ministry of exampleship. Mature believers should be setting the standards for those who are less spiritually experienced. Leadership in a local church is a shared responsibility; the pastor cannot succeed in bringing his flock to maturity if he labors alone. For us there is no authorized priestly class, like the Levitical priesthood of the Old Testament. The New Testament order of apostles and prophets has also passed from the scene. Today we are a "knit together" band of believers who depend upon one another for edification, each one taking the lead where needed (Colossians 2:19; Ephesians 2:19-22; 4:16).

The role of the old women teaching the young

---

[6] This is the only New Testament occurrence of *sōtērios*. Septuagint usage of *sōtērios,-n* falls generally under one of two headings: 1) anything which yields or brings rescue, salvation or preservation; or 2) technical term for the peace-offering.

women to be virtuous wives, mothers and homemakers (Titus 2:4-5) is an important factor in the stability of the church. This teaching duty for women supplements the men's duty to exercise overall spiritual authority in the household of God (1 Timothy 2:12).

A consequence of Christians not living up to the standard of sound teaching is to bring blasphemy (Titus 2:5) and condemnation (2:8) against the word of God, and evil speech against its followers (2:8). The world is only too happy to make light of the gospel on our account. Therefore we should be attempting to make our lives shine forth as adornments of our Saviour's teaching (2:10). The Saviour's teaching referred to here is not the direct quotes of the Lord Jesus' words in the four Gospels and Acts, because there He is revealed as a minister of the circumcision (Romans 15:8). Rather it is the teaching Christ entrusted to the Apostle Paul for our benefit in this dispensation of His grace (Ephesians 3:1-9).

To adorn this teaching with a worthy walk (Ephesians 4:1) is only reasonable, in view of the saving grace that has been given us (Titus 2:10).

God's "salvation-bringing" (literal sense of *sōtērios* in 2:11[7]) is for all men, but sadly not all will receive it. *Sōtērios* is the adjectival form (masculine gender) of the noun *sōtēria* ("salvation"), and here it is used substantively (i.e., as a noun). The same adjective in neuter gender (*sōtērion*) is also used substantively in a passage suggestive of Titus:

> Be it known to you therefore, that this <u>saving instrument</u> of God is sent to the nations and they will hear [it].   (Acts 28:28)

In Acts the saving agent is the gospel sent nation-ward. Such a gospel certainly heralds God's grace in offering salvation to a lost world.

One Calling or Two?

Although both Acts 28 and Titus 2 deal with salvation in rather basic terms, we should question whether the Bible really teaches a basic salvation apart from some specific hope, calling and inheritance. My view is that the specific hope,

---

[7] *Seed & Bread*, No. 8, O. Sellers.

calling and inheritance were implied throughout the letter to Titus, as both the writer and first readers were already well acquainted with them.

Some have seen in Acts 28:28 a basic form of salvation passing through to the new dispensation. According to this view, Paul had two distinct gospel messages for this dispensation. He taught a basic salvation in addition to the new revelation of a heavenly calling (revealed to him some time after Acts 28). They believe the message of John's Gospel also embodies the teaching of this basic salvation (e.g., John 3:16), a teaching which carried through to our dispensation[8].

Some others, who hold with the conventional view of a late date of authorship for John's Gospel (90-95 A.D.), propose not only two distinct messages but two concurrent callings of Christians today: one basic and earthly, the other dispensational and heavenly. But this position seems to contradict the "one hope of your calling" set forth in Ephesians

---

[8] Ephesians, Philippians, Colossians, 1 Timothy, 2 Timothy, Titus, and Philemon.

4:4. If a separate calling of basic faith Christians exists apart from the church of the one body, then the earthly group could only reap confusion from reading Paul's Mystery Epi

stles[9] (especially Ephesians and Colossians). If God has called two concurrent companies of believers, then He needs to communicate with them more effectively than He has done so far. It seems that the belief in two callings amounts to an attempt to explain, and perhaps to justify, the divided state of Christianity. But why stop at two callings when there are so many more divisions? It may be that separation into two church bodies is emotionally satisfying because it divides the Christian world neatly into two camps: "us" and "them." But this fortress mentality is itself divisive and ought to be avoided by thoughtful Christians.

There is no firm Scriptural basis for a dual calling theory today; it rests on inference and analogy of an ambiguous sort. Some would draw an analogy from

---

[9] However, *âshar* – to declare happy – is used of God (e.g., Psalm 72:17).

Old Testament times when God divided mankind into two groups: Israel His elect, and the rest of the nations. When they followed the dictates of conscience, the nations were also accepted of God (Romans 2:14-16). Although they were excluded from Israel's temporal inheritance, they might share in their eternal inheritance (Matthew 8:5-12).

We are unable to classify Christians as to their being first or second tier in God's program of election, but the ability to discern profitable from unprofitable servants does seem to be germane to our topic (e.g., see the parable of the talents in Matthew 25:14-30). This is a sounder model to use if we feel we must take the measure of a fellow Christian. Our attitude toward those whom we perceive to be in error ought to be helpful and forbearing, rather than railing and accusatory. After having preached the truth, rightly divided, we may find ourselves disapproved if we fail to walk in love (1 Corinthians 9:27; Ephesians 5:1-2).

The Epiphanies

Another main theme of the Pastoral Epistles concerns the "appearing" (*epiphaneia*, literally "shining forth") of the Lord Jesus Christ. At least two separate events, one past and one future, are referred to as His "appearing". Titus 2:11-13 brings the two events together in a single text.

> For the grace of God appeared (*epiphainō*) as a salvation-bringer for all men, instructing us that having denied ungodliness and worldly passions we should live prudently and righteously and godly in the present age, awaiting the happy hope, even the <u>appearing</u> (*epiphaneia*) of the glory of the great God, even our Saviour Christ Jesus. (Titus 2:11-13)

In our Lord's first appearing He manifested saving grace to men by means of His vicarious death and resurrection. Because we have been saved, we are admonished to live prudently in the present age anticipating the next appearing of the Saviour. On first glance the earlier of the two epiphanies seems to refer only to the death, resurrection and ascension aspects of Christ's incarnation. If the passage teaches only the basic aspects of salvation, then those must be the events indicated. But there is more to this *epiphaneia* than meets the eye.

The saving work which the Lord accomplished during His incarnation was restricted first to Jews, then later during Acts to Jews and a limited number of neighboring Greeks. It did not apply to "all men" universally until the ushering in of "the dispensation of the Mystery" (Ephesians 3:9). Now He is truly accessible to all men, regardless of race, tribe or nation. So the first appearing seems at least to include the initial revelation of the Mystery, which itself relates back to a hidden purpose behind the cross and empty tomb of Christ.

There are some texts in Ephesians and Colossians that deal with this first *epiphaneia*. In Ephesians 4:8-12 Christ is described as having ascended into the height, giving gifts to men. In His ascension "far above all the heavens, so that He might fill all these things", He also led captivity captive. The context of the gifts is the edification of the body of Christ (vv.12-13). These events took place at the outset of the dispensation of the Mystery – not the resurrection-ascension recorded in the Gospels and Acts. Coinciding with this is Christ's spoliation and triumph over the principalities and powers in Colossians 2:15. These were events close to our home!

Another passage amplifying the first *epiphaneia* is found in 2 Timothy.

> Therefore you should not be ashamed of the testimony of our Lord nor of me His prisoner; but suffer evil for the gospel's sake according to the power of God, Who saved us and called us with a holy calling, not according to our works, but according to His own purpose and grace which was given to us in Christ Jesus before age-times, but manifested (*phaneroō*, the root word in *epiphaneia*) now by the appearing (*epiphaneia*) of our Saviour Christ Jesus, Who destroyed death and brought to light life and incorruption by the gospel, unto which I was appointed a herald and apostle and teacher of nations. (2 Timothy 1:8-11)

What gospel, or "good news", does Paul refer to here? For what gospel message was Paul appointed a "herald and apostle and teacher of nations"? The Jews and Israel are not even mentioned here (or anywhere in the letter in a positive vein), so this gospel must apply to the post Acts 28 period. God's purpose and grace toward His people, according to this gospel, predate the age-times. These times coincide with the church's election in Christ before the foundation (overthrow) of the world (Ephesians 1:3). The "holy calling", "life" and "incorruption" He now offers constitute in general terms the good news for us today. With all these things drawn into the context we can hardly equate the first *epiphaneia* to Christ's earthly sojourn. It must define His bringing to light our holy calling, as revealed in the later epistles of Paul.

The revelation of the Mystery began with Paul (Ephesians 3:2-3), and he alone was privileged to transmit the Scriptures regarding it - these are the Mystery Epistles. Paul was also privileged to see and hear the Lord in His present glory on a number of occasions (Acts 26:16). One of the last occasions (if not the very last) fell after Acts 28, and the revelation of the Mystery accompanied it. Whether the Lord appeared before his eyes physically or in a trance or in a still small voice to his mind is not known, but we are unable to dissociate the *epiphaneia* from this act of revelation to His foundation ministers (Ephesians 2:20).

There remains a final Biblical reference to the first appearing.

But when the kindness and love toward man
of our Saviour God appeared (*epiphainō*).
(Titus 3:4)

God's kindness and love toward man reached their
epitome in the present dispensation of His grace.
Before the close of Acts, God's dealings with man
were governed by the terms of various covenants.
The covenants defined privileged relationships
between God and various groups of people, and they
represented God's graciousness toward them. All
that said, the covenants also had conditions attached
and grievous covenant breakers were liable to divine
punishments. The covenants were not the high water
mark of God's kindness and love.

His greatest beneficence was manifested not at the
cross (although it certainly was a blessing hidden
there) but about 33 years later in Paul's hired house
(Acts 28:30-31) where the Lord revealed to him the
greatness of   this dispensation of grace. In this
dispensation we receive only blessings from God
(Ephesians 1:3), not judgments. It is no longer
appropriate for us to pray, "forgive us our sins as we
also have forgiven those who sin against us..."
(Matthew 6:12), but rather that we be "forgiving

each other, just as God in Christ has also forgiven" us (Ephesians 4:32).

Now let us return to Titus 2:13 and "the happy hope". This phrase seems to indicate a rather specific expectation on the part of believers and not some basic resurrection belief resulting from a basic salvation. If the subject of the text were basic salvation, where would such a hope be realized? Those who recognize that God's "purpose of the ages" proceeds from a manifold plan (Ephesians 3:10-11) will recognize that this is not a trivial question. In every dispensation, those who believe God are saved *from* sin and death *for* eternal life. But that eternal life will be experienced in a manner peculiar to one's hope and calling.

Israel's place of blessing will be in the earth during the millennium, and afterwards in the New Jerusalem which will descend to earth (Hebrews 12:22; Revelation 20:6; 21:2-4). But the multinational church, the body of Christ, will be blessed in the heavenly places at the right hand of the Father (Ephesians 1:3; 19-20). A basic salvation doctrine is common to both spheres of blessing, but we must proceed beyond that. Something more than the basics also applies. In every instance in Scripture, whether expressed or implied, there is a place and circumstance appropriate for eternal life to be lived. After all, we will not be like God in His spiritual omnipresence; we require some place to call "home."

The "happy hope" of Titus must either be the hope of Israel and the earthly families of nations (Genesis 12:1-3) or the heavenly hope belonging to the church today. Because the book of Titus deals with a post-Acts church, we should look to Paul's prison epistles (principally Ephesians and Colossians) for amplification on any basic themes that appear in Titus.

The "happy hope" in Titus 2:13 is best read with an apposition following: "even the appearing of the glory of our great God and Saviour Jesus Christ". Our hope and Christ's future appearing are inseparably bound. It seems this hope is not ours alone, for God also calls Himself "happy" in connection with it.

> ... and if any other thing is opposed to the sound teaching according to the gospel of the

glory of the <u>happy</u> God, which I was entrusted with. (1 Timothy 1:10-11)

... keep the commandment spotless, irreproachable until the appearing (*epiphaneia*) of our Lord Jesus Christ, which He will show in its own seasons, the *happy* and only Sovereign, the King of those who reign, the Lord of those who rule, Who alone has immortality, dwelling in unapproachable light. (1 Timothy 6:14-16)

These two passages are remarkable because nowhere else in the Bible is God described as "happy" (whether *makarios* in the New Testament and Septuagint, or *ashrêy* in the Hebrew Old Testament[10]). Surely this future shining forth of the Lord is a pivotal event in God's plan of the ages. Both His happiness and ours are dependent on it.

Our understanding of the future epiphany of Christ can be broadened by material from other texts.

---

[10] Mistranslated "saints" in Eph.1:18; 2:19 and Col.1:12 (*KJV*).

If then you were raised with Christ, seek the things above where Christ is sitting at the right hand of God. Be mindful of the things above, not the things on the earth. For you died, and your life has been hidden with Christ in God. When Christ our life may be manifested (*phaneroō*), then also will you be manifested (*phaneroō*) with Him in glory. (Colossians 3:1-4)

Because the emphasis here is on "things above", it appears that Christ's manifesting and the church's resurrection will be witnessed only in the heavenly sphere. No bodies need rise out of the earth for this heavenly translation to occur. Indeed, in spirit we are already raised and seated there at the Father's right hand, and already translated into His heavenly kingdom (Ephesians 2:6; Colossians 1:13). The expression "in glory" in the quote above might also be translated "in the Glory", this being equivalent to the heavenly "Holies"[11] referred to in the Mystery Epistles. The "Holies" are located in the

---

[11] Ephesians 1:3,20; 2:6; 3:10 and 6:12.

"heavenlies"[12], typically translated "heavenly places" by the *KJV*.

The happy hope is further described by 2 Timothy 4:1,8 and 18, which link the *epiphaneia* with Christ's heavenly kingdom and His sitting in judgment of the church. Whether the *epiphaneia* of the Pastoral Epistles bears any relationship to the prophetic "day of the Lord" is difficult to say for sure. There are two suggestive references which do pertain to the day of the Lord.

> ... and then will be revealed the lawless one, whom the Lord Jesus will slay with the breath of His mouth and destroy with the shining forth (*epiphaneia*) of His coming (*parousia*). (2 Thessalonians 2:8)

> ... and I will give wonders in the heaven above and signs upon the earth below, blood and fire and vapor of smoke. The sun will be turned into darkness and the moon into blood before the great and shining (*epiphanēs*) day of the

---

[12] 1 Timothy 1:5; 2 Timothy 2:22.

Lord comes. (Acts 2:19-20)

Note that in 2 Thessalonians it is not just His *epiphaneia*, but the *epiphaneia* of His *parousia* ("official presence") that is described. But His *parousia* will be on earth, not in heavenly places. Although Israel and the church are expecting two different hopes, the shared use of the word *epiphaneia* may indicate a compound event. A heavenly epiphany involving the church, leading directly into an earthly epiphany in the day of the Lord, may be inferred from these texts. Just as the first *epiphaneia* may be understood as a progressive process during the foundation period of the Mystery, so the second *epiphaneia* might also take place as a series of events.

On Redemption, Citizenship and Good Works

The Saviour Whose shining forth we await so expectantly is the same One Who redeemed us for Himself (Titus 2:14). The terms used in the Epistle to Titus to express this redemption may at first glance seem to have a Jewish flavor. For example, the redemption is a freeing from "lawlessness" and it is able to "purify" a "peculiar people", who become "zealous" of "good works". The Greek words involved are all closely connected with Israel's covenants (through the Septuagint Old Testament). "Lawlessness" prompts us to think of the Law of Moses and its hundreds of precepts. However, New Testament usage of *anomia* is directed to the moral law rather than the ritual elements of the Law of Moses. For example, long before the revelation of the Law, Sodom and Gomorrah practiced lawless deeds (2 Peter 2:8). Nor does God's moral law vanish at redemption, but becomes written on the heart of "the new man" (Ephesians 4:24). And the purification of the church (Ephesians 5:25-26) does not yield a ritual purity, as under the Law. But true purity flourishes because the new man is created in the image of Christ, Who is pure of any sin or taint of corruption. A "pure heart"[13] and "pure conscience"[14] belong to him who purges himself of the ritualistic elements of Judaism

---

[13] 1 Timothy 3:9; 2 Timothy 1:3.

[14] Ephesians 1:7, 18; 2:7; 3:8, 16; Philippians 4:19; Colossians 1:27; 2:2.

(Titus 1:14-16; Colossians 2:20-23). Those who seek the outmoded purity of legalism will be disapproved as to every good work, whatever their zeal.

The phrase "peculiar people" (*laos periousios*) appears in the New Testament only in Titus. But it is found five times in the Old Testament, always used of Israel. Interestingly, the "peculiar people" of 1 Peter 2:9 is a different expression entirely (*laos eis peripoēsin*).

It should be observed in Acts 15:14 that the Gentile converts of that time also became "a people" of God. And elsewhere Paul uses the conversion of "not My people" to "My people" of Hosea 1:9-10 to them (Romans 9:25-26). The church, the body of Christ, is not referred to directly as a "people" except in Titus.

However, the fellow citizenship of the saints as contrasted with "the commonwealth of Israel" (Ephesians 2:19,12) and the heavenly citizenship we possess (Philippians 3:20) are certainly the attributes of a distinct people. So the words "peculiar people" should not be understood as a description of Israel only. It is a generic term that applies to various families of God's elect. Furthermore, *Thayer* gives definitions of "riches" and "wealth" to the related noun, *periousia*. Israel were promised riches of basket and store. The body of Christ has spiritual wealth.[15] Both Israel and the body of Christ are peoples of riches – but the nature of the riches differ!

In the Greek Old Testament God is occasionally described with the word *zēlotēs*, usually translated "jealous". Another sense of the word is zealous or fervent, and this should be our attitude toward the good works that God has prepared for us to perform (Ephesians 2:10; Colossians 1:10). One example of zealous works is cited in Colossians 4:12-13 where Epaphras is said to have agonized in prayer for the Colossian saints. Although there is parallel terminology in the books of Moses, legalism is not what Paul is getting at in the latter part of Titus chapter 2.

At the end of chapter 2 Paul summarizes his instructions to Titus thus far with an exhortation.

---

[15] *Loutron*, literally a "wash-pot".

These things speak and exhort and convict with all command. Let no one despise you. (Titus 2:15)

Titus seems to have enjoyed a high degree of authority as a Christ appointed minister of the gospel. As with the relatively youthful Timothy (1 Timothy 4:11-12), Titus was to let no challenge to his authority go unchecked. Paul's warnings here and in 2:8 imply that challengers were beginning to appear, and they were to be dealt with decisively. Eventually such challenges would be the undoing of Paul's ministry in some areas, such as the Roman province of Asia (2 Timothy 1:15).

Titus
Chapter 3

Titus Chapter 3

All the chapter divisions in the Bible were put there by man, and this one is not particularly well placed. It would have been more logical to start chapter 3 at 2:15, because the thoughts from 2:15 to 3:2 are progressive. Here Paul reminded Titus of his duty to "speak and exhort and convict". In carrying out this duty, Titus was to remind the church of their duties, including subordination to authority.

The "principalities and powers" in 3:1 are not the heavenly variety, with whom we have a continual, spiritual wrestling (Ephesians 6:12). These are earthly authorities. The specific type of authority (civil or ecclesiastic) is not indicated here, but the reference to "all men" at the end of 3:2 would seem to demand that all types of authority are meant. The same or similar Greek terms (*archē*, *archon*, *exousia*) are used elsewhere both of religious authorities in the synagogue (Luke 12:11) and of civil authorities (Romans 13:1-7).

During the transition from apostolic to pastoral authority at the beginning of this dispensation, the church had ministers of the gospel who were appointed by Christ Himself. These men exercised a degree of authority in the church that is not seen today. Those who take to themselves such authority nowadays are false apostles. There was an orderliness in the early church based in part upon this apostolic authority (Colossians 2:5; 1 Corinthians 16:15-16). In addition to obedience to these spiritual authorities, the saints were to be subordinated to both Christ and one another (Ephesians 5:24,21). All our obedience derives ultimately from our allegiance and obedience to Christ.

One might question whether for conscience sake we ought to disobey civil authorities on some occasions. Certainly the Bible provides us many examples of men who chose to obey God rather than men. See Acts 5:27-29, for example. The Scripture does not teach us to obey immoral or unjust laws enacted by earthly authorities, rather that we be prepared to suffer some injustice in this life. If we return good for evil it will promote the gospel of Christ our Lord. There is no more powerful example of the subordination of the just to the unjust than in the life of Jesus Christ. He had no sin and did only good for man, but He suffered much at the hands of men.

An additional reason for Paul's emphasis on submission to authority may have been the coming of persecution. Possibly this persecution had already begun. But even if it was as yet unforeseen by Christians, certainly God knew what sort of malice Nero would inflict on Roman Christians in 64 A.D. Both then and during later outbreaks of persecution the honor of Christ would be well served by blameless and orderly followers. Doubtless some bystanders of the persecution would note the stark contrast between the moral Christian life and the depravity into which Roman morals had sunk. Thus the way would be paved for some to respond to the goodness of the Lord.

Submission, coupled with gentleness and meekness (Titus 3:2), speaks powerfully of the goodness of Christ. Paul goes on to compare this desirable lifestyle with the manner of life he once shared with his fellow Jews: thoughtless, disobedient, deceived, craven, malicious, envious and hateful (3:3). Out of this pit of corruption Christ had lifted up Paul and other Jewish believers. He had done this out of kindness, and not because of any good deeds they had done (3:4-5). Although Paul could claim that his keeping of the Law had been blameless (Philippians 3:6,9), his righteousness in the Law had still left him in the awful state described in Titus 3:3. It took the pouring out of a spiritual baptism of renewal for him to learn about God's saving mercy. A baptism like that described in Colossians 2:12-13 and Ephesians 5:26 was needed to regenerate him, because none of the ritual baptisms of the Law could do it. The "water[16]" in Titus 3:5 is the very word and spirit of God, and corresponds to the "living water" of John 4:10-14. With regeneration comes justification and inheritance and hope.

Profitable and Unprofitable Works

In 3:8 Paul exhorted Titus to affirm strongly the faithful word he was sharing with him. As Titus promoted that word, faithful men would profit from it and become mindful of the good works prepared for them to perform (Ephesians 2:10). Boldness in performing these works was the expectation: "in

---

[16] From the Father emanated the "Potencies", from whom came the angels and then all the lower orders of material creation including man.

order that they who have believed God may take thought to <u>stand forward</u> in good works." Of course faith is the necessary prerequisite for good works. Paul repeats the command to boldly pursue good works in verse 14, but here it reads a little differently.

> And let our own also learn to take thought to stand forward in good works for necessary wants, lest they be unfruitful.

Whom does Paul mean by "our own" here? The immediate context seems to limit it to Paul's own circle of associates, such as Artemas, Tychicus, Zenas, Apollos, and even Titus. Referring to the structural diagram on an earlier page we shall find the remote context supplied by 1:5-8 with its criteria for selecting elders. The phrase "our own" would seem to include all of the leadership; and we see that the command to "stand forward" applies to them also. The promotion of faithful men into church leadership, whether by the Holy Spirit or by the hand of man, was certainly not to be used as an excuse for complacency. The same high standards of conduct apply to all. To whom more is given, more is to be expected.

The good works of verse 8 stand in contrast with the unprofitable works of verse 9 "mindless inquiries and genealogies and strifes and contentions about Law". Although they appear as separate items, the four things mentioned above are related to one another. Mindless inquiries ("moronic debates" might be a better translation), including genealogical speculations, will lead to disputes and legalistic wrangling in the end. These speculative inquiries call to mind the worst aspects of the rabbinical discourses, which we know led many Jews astray into the "commandments of men" (Matthew 15:1-9).

We should not limit this subject to rabbinism only. The Jews kept good genealogical records for their people, so there was probably not much speculation over their "genealogies." In the Greek world, however, there was a marked tendency toward metaphysical speculation, particularly on the origin and generation of the various orders of creation[17].

---

[17] Cf. *Ecclesiastical History*, Eusebius, book 3, chapter 4, and *Apostolic Constitutions*, book 7, chapter 46, both dating from about the fourth century.

The fantastic theories of the first and second centuries A.D. that became known as "Gnostic" had their ideological origin in the philosophical activity of Pythagoreans, Platonists and Stoics who predated Christ. The Jewish philosopher Philo became a Hellenizer of Jewish dogma and may have influenced later Jewish Gnostics, such as the author of *The Apocalypse of Adam*. Similarly, some who fell away from Christianity would later import Christian concepts into these speculative systems. One such person may have been Simon Magus, who attempted to buy spiritual powers from the Apostle Peter (Acts 8:5-24). Irenaeus credits him with being the father of Gnosticism (*Against Heresies*, II, Preface), but this certainly gives too much blame to one man. The Greco-Roman world was awash in philosophy and superstition. No doubt a backslidden Christian had many corrupt options to choose from, if he sought an easier course.

Titus was to distance himself from all such speculators and their unprofitable discourse, and after several warnings he was to reject anyone practicing sectarian strife (Titus 3:11). Paul teaches that sectarianism is sin, and appears to put us on the horns of a dilemma. The evil of sectarianism exists today and one is justified in rejecting a "Christian" who holds fast to and spreads fundamentally flawed doctrine.

However, we should bear in mind that to the untutored and unconverted even a justifiable rejection will itself appear as mere sectarianism. As long as the holder of such doctrine is not "overthrowing whole houses", then we would do better to reject only the doctrine. Through God's graciousness and our patient endurance, those who are in error (whether it be mild or grievous) might be persuaded to reconsider their thinking (2 Timothy 2:24-26). We no longer have apostolic authorities to settle all differences of interpretation and practice. And certainly we ought to be able to bear with one another when we disagree on minor points of doctrine.

Conclusion

Conclusion

Titus was an early and dearly beloved associate of Paul's, but he appears to have gone his own way in the end. The tradition that holds Titus to have been "first bishop" of Crete is not very credible, because Titus' mission there was apostolic or evangelistic and not pastoral. See Appendix B for more on this issue.

Although the Pauline authorship of Titus has been repudiated by the "higher critical" school of theology, their arguments for a late date are unconvincing. Their principal reason for dismissing Paul as the author is based on word usage and writing style. But this position presumes an intimate knowledge of Paul's mind and vocabulary, and is too thin a basis to conclude fraud. And fraud it would be too, because the writer identifies himself as the Apostle Paul. If fraudulent, the Pastoral Epistles might still be of interest to philologists and historians but Christians need not take them seriously as doctrine.

As for dating the epistle, none of the personal details

fits into the Acts chronology. Nor does Paul's attitude toward Judaism in Titus accord with the Acts period. Missing are the need to minister to Jew first and the willingness to conduct oneself as a Jew when dealing with Jews. Also, Paul's two years of house arrest must have concluded before the Neronian persecution began in 64 A.D. It is impossible to fix dates to Paul's return and subsequent journeys about the Aegean region, but a time between 63 and 68 A.D. seems reasonable. Paul's need for Zenas the lawyer and Apollos the orator is a signal that points toward his final imprisonment, which is evident in 2 Timothy.

Looking at Titus in overview, the central portion of the book highlights the perennial conflict between flesh and spirit. This can be seen in what the righteous work of Christ accomplished in overcoming the sinful works of man. This conflict is also mirrored in the resistance to sound doctrine by those preferring a carnal Christianity.

Chapter One

In chapter one we noted how generalized the epistle's characterizations of doctrine ("the faith") are. Doctrine in Titus is preeminently practical in scope and application. Few definitive statements of foundational or dispensational truth can be found in the Pastorals, because such teaching is left for other books to develop. One could go to John's Gospel and Romans for foundation doctrines, such as the deity of Christ, and our salvation and justification in Him. Ephesians and Colossians are required for current dispensational teaching, such as our freedom from Israel's covenants and our hope in "heavenly places". The main thrust of the message in Titus is the working out of salvation. A worked out salvation will be evident in the godly attitude and reverence of believers, whatever their position in the church.

Paul's attitude toward Judaism in the final verses of chapter one help give the book its dispensational coloring. There is no accommodation of Judaism here, so Israel as the elect nation must have been absent from God's dealings with men at this time.

Chapter Two

In chapter two we find an emphasis on healthy teaching and healthy faith. One of the needful components of any health program is exercise, and this also applies to the "sound teaching" and "sound faith" aspects of the Pastorals. Knowledge of the word of God, acquired through study, is necessary first (analogous to nourishment for the body). Then in order to mature, a nourished faith must become an exercised faith. To do less is to cling to a dead faith (James 2:26; Ephesians 2:10). In applying the sound teaching to various groups, the Epistle suggests an affinity between old men generally and those appointed as elders in the church. Older believers, by virtue of greater spiritual experience, should be taking the lead in their churches and helping the elders with their pastoring responsibilities.

Although the Epistle discusses salvation in rather simplistic terms, we should not conclude that its readers were unskilled in fathoming the deep things of God. Apparently they were well enough grounded in foundational and dispensational truths not to require additional lessons in them in a letter devoted almost wholly to practical issues. This leaves us with some difficulty in placing Titus dispensationally. It is not obvious whether the salvation hope of believers is earthly or heavenly. We can make dispensational inferences about this book based on God's promise "before age-times"

(1:2) and the unequivocally anti-Judaistic tone (1:14-16), coupled with historical details that do not fit into the Acts period.

We examined the term *epiphaneia* at length and found that it covers multiple Biblical events. The Pastoral Epistles' use of the term applies principally to the later revelation given to the Apostle Paul (the heavenly hope of the church). *Epiphaneia* has broader applications, however, and it may also relate to the second coming of Christ.

Chapter Three

Chapter 3 begins with a commendation of obedience. We should subordinate ourselves to all types of authority, as long as they do not contravene God's moral order. In doing so we shall put our Christian faith in the best possible light and not give it a bad name.

The chapter concludes with an emphasis on good works and diligence. In all his letters Paul discouraged a lazy and unprofitable faith, while encouraging a vigorous outworking of salvation. The good works of a fruitful walk stand in contrast with the unprofitable works of sectarianism: fractious debates, speculations and legalistic contentions. We walk a difficult line today in trying to judge whether to reject "the sectarian man" or to forbear and try to teach him. A good rule to use would be to practice forbearance until other believers begin to be led astray from fundamental doctrine.

The last few verses in Titus give us a picture of the orderly state then present in the church. Artemas or Tychicus would soon be under orders to relieve Titus, who was to meet with Paul at Nicopolis. Zenas and Apollos had already been summoned and Titus was to speed them on their journey. The church leadership seems to have possessed a military style of discipline; no one disdained subordinating himself to spiritual authority. With the passing of these apostles and evangelists our spiritual world has become much more ambiguous. To keep our focus we need to seek guidance continually from our Lord and Head, Jesus Christ, because He is the ultimate Authority.

Appendix A: Godliness in the Pastoral Epistles

Appendix A: Godliness in the Pastoral Epistles

A^1.	1 Tim 2:2	that we may lead a tranquil life in all **godliness** and dignity
B.	3:15-16	confessedly great is the mystery of **godliness**: God was manifested in flesh (of His saints, that is) ...
C.a.	4:7	exercise yourself as to **godliness**
b.	4:8	for bodily exercise is profitable for a little while, but **godliness** is profitable for everything
D.	6:3	sound words ... of our Lord Jesus Christ, even the teaching according to **godliness**
C.a.	6:5	men ... destitute of truth, holding **godliness** to be gain
b.	6:6	but **godliness** with contentment is great tain
A^2.	6:11	flee these things and pursue righteousness, **godliness**, faith,

		love
B.	2 Timothy 3:5	having a form of **godliness** but denying the power of it
A¹.	3:12	all who want to live **godly** in Christ Jesus will be pressured
D.	Titus 1:1	recognition of truth which is according to **godliness**
A².	2:12	having denied ungodliness and worldly passions we should live discreetly and righteously and **godly** in the present age

Summary

A1   Quiet life in godliness to be desired, but godly life in conflict rather to be expected.

B   The mystery of godliness (in-worked power) contrasted with the mystery of iniquity (power denied)
The profit or gain of godliness contrasted with the profit of the flesh.

D   Teaching or truth which is "according to godliness"

A2   Flee the old life of sin and pursue the new life that is righteous and godly.

Appendix B: The Role of Bishops and Elders

Appendix B:
The Role of Bishops and Elders

When we read the words "bishop" and "deacon" in the Bible we tend to invest them with our modern notions of what a bishop and a deacon are. But with a little Scripture searching we shall find that the bishops and deacons of apostolic times were quite different from their spiritual successors. What we see today is an unwarranted aggrandizement of the offices, and the separation of an authoritarian "clergy" into a priestly class. It was not so in the beginning.

Several centuries after Paul, church tradition held Titus to be the first bishop of Crete[18]. This tradition appears to have been based upon his mission as described in his Epistle, particularly the commission to appoint elders in every Cretan city. The Epistle's subscription first appeared in a ninth century manuscript and is usually omitted from our English Bibles:

To Titus, chosen first bishop of the Cretan church, written from Nicopolis of Macedonia.

The description "first" may refer either to rank or time. The concept of a bishop who is first in rank is really that of an archbishop or general overseer, and is not a scriptural bishop at all. Titus was left in Crete to appoint bishops (pl.), for this is the role of the "elders" he was to select. In Acts 19 Paul had referred to the leaders of the Ephesian church as both "elders" (*presbuteroi*, v.17) and "overseers" (*episkopoi*, v.28, elsewhere translated "bishops" in the *KJV*). He instructed them to "feed" (*poimainō*, v.28, meaning to "shepherd") the "flock" (*poimnion*), and this was typically the job of a "shepherd" or "pastor" (*poimēn*). Therefore we can conclude that the leadership titles "elder", "overseer", "bishop", "pastor" and "shepherd" are all equivalent, and we should add "teacher" to the list because a "bishop" should be "apt to teach" (1 Timothy 3:1-2).

None of these terms was new to the New Testament; they had a long Old Testament tradition through the Septuagint Greek text. For example, there were the seventy elders who helped Moses to judge Israel in the wilderness (Numbers 11:16-17), and at a later time the elders of the Sanhedrin disputed what to do about Jesus. The overseers, or "officers", led the armies of Israel dating back from Moses' time (Numbers 31:14). Later, overseers in the Temple supervised the work of restoration (2 Chronicles 34:10-12). Israel's need for a pastor ("shepherd") also dates from Moses' day (Numbers 27:15-18).

From the beginning of His covenant with the nation of Israel, God Himself became their teacher through Moses (Deuteronomy 6:1). At a later time when that Prophet like unto Moses visited them, He went about teaching the people (Matthew 7:28-29; 11:1). The need for God's people to be taught and led has remained a universal need, although the manner of their oversight has varied with the changes of dispensation.

The position of "pastor" is one of the Biblical categories of spiritual leader for our dispensation. Ephesians 4:11 lists apostles, prophets, evangelists, and pastors and teachers. The apostles and prophets belong to the church's foundation period (Ephesians 2:20), and they have long since passed from the scene. "Pastors and teachers" may be better translated as "pastors, even teachers" in view of the teaching requirement for pastors (1 Timothy 3:2). In addition to the four categories found in Ephesians, 1 Timothy adds the "deacon" or "minister" (*diakonos*), whose role seems to be to assist the pastor in his duties (1 Timothy 3:8-13; Philippians 1:1). There is no scriptural basis for more of a leadership hierarchy than this. Those who exercised authority over pastors were the Christ appointed apostles and evangelists, not archbishops.

Let us return now to the matter of Titus as "first bishop of the Cretan church." When Titus arrived in Crete, Christians were already to be found there, and one may assume that their churches had people taking the spiritual lead (i.e., pastoring). We have also noted that there is no Biblical support for the appointment of archbishops during apostolic times. Therefore it seems unlikely that Titus could have been "first bishop" of Crete in either sense of the word "first". The later subscription to the Epistle is either an attempt to legitimize a later institution or is merely a reflection of later conditions in a church no longer following the apostolic model.

A dispensational distinction about the appointment

of elders can be drawn between Titus and earlier accounts like those in Ephesians and Acts. In Titus 1:5-9, as in 1 Timothy 3:1-7 and 5:22, the traits of a prospective elder are spelled out clearly because human judgment would be at work in the selection process. Previously, however, it was revealed that "pastors and teachers" were Christ-appointed (Ephesians 4:11-12). Earlier still they were said to be appointed by the Holy Spirit (Acts 20:28). This evidence puts Titus very late in the Pauline ministry, even after his initial teaching on the present dispensation in Ephesians and Colossians. Thus, Titus must also have been written for our special benefit today.

More on Titus

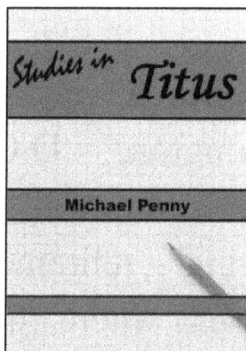

About the author

Glen Burch was born in Washington, D.C., in 1947, and is at present enjoying retirement in Virginia where he is a teacher at Grace Bible Church of Hampton Roads. After high school, and his time in the army, he held several positions before becoming a civilian analyst with the U.S. Navy, a position he held for many years.

Also by Glen Burch

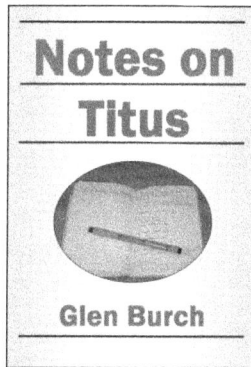

The Mystery of Godliness

Tithing and other gifts

Abraham's Progress in the Covenant of God

Notes on Titus

Please note:

Further details of all the books mentioned can be
seen on **www.obt.org.uk**

The can be ordered from the website
and also from

The Open Bible Trust,
Fordland Mount, Upper Basildon,
Reading, RG8 8LU, UK.

They are also available as eBooks
from Amazon and Apple,
and also as KDP paperbacks from Amazon.

Search Magazine

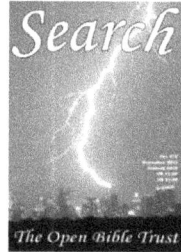

For a free sample of
The Open Bible Trust's magazine Search,
please email

admin@obt.org.uk

or visit

www.obt.org.uk/search

About this book

Notes on Titus

Paul's letter to Titus, together with 1 and 2 Timothy, form what are commonly called the Pastoral Epistles., They were first called 'Pastoral' in the 18th century and were given this label because they emphasise the responsibilities of a 'pastor'.

However, it may be more accurate to call them *Leadership Epistles*, because 'leadership' is addressed in them on many fronts; for example … personal, parental, spousal, generational, pastoral, evangelistic and apostolic.

As a result we will all benefit from Glen Burch's exposition of Paul's letter to Titus.

Publications of The Open Bible Trust must be in accordance with its evangelical, fundamental and dispensational basis. However, beyond this minimum, writers are free to express whatever beliefs they may have as their own understanding, provided that the aim in so doing is to further the object of The Open Bible Trust. A copy of the doctrinal basis is available at

www.obt.org.uk/doctrinal-basis

or from:

The Open Bible Trust
Fordland Mount, Upper Basildon,
Reading, RG8 8LU, UK.

www.ingramcontent.com/pod-product-compliance
Lightning Source LLC
Chambersburg PA
CBHW062114040426
42337CB00042B/2159